Present Poets 2
Scotland to the World to Scotland

Present Poets 2

Scotland to the World, the World to Scotland

POEMS OF ARRIVAL AND
DEPARTURE COMPILED BY
JENNI CALDER

NMS Publishing

Published by NMS Publishing Limited, Royal Museum,
Chambers Street, Edinburgh EH1 1JF

Collection © NMS Publishing Limited and the poets 1999

Information about our books is available at www.nms.ac.uk

British Library Cataloguing in Publication Data
A catalogue record of this book is available from the British Library

ISBN 1 901663 39 6

Designed by NMS Publishing
Printed in the United Kingdom by Cambridge University Press,
Printing Division

Cover illustration: Lynn Mercer

THE SCOTTISH **ARTS** COUNCIL

Contents

SCOTLAND TO THE WORLD TO SCOTLAND

Between 1996 and 1998 fifty poems were displayed as posters on the hoardings that surrounded the building site of the new Museum of Scotland. The poems, all specially written for the project by poets from all over Scotland and beyond, ranged over many aspects of Scotland's past and present. The new museum opened to the public on 1 December 1998, and the poems were published in a volume called *Present Poets*.

The response to both the posters and the volume was so enthusiastic that the NMS decided to run a second poetry project. The theme this time reflected an initiative newly launched by the NMS, Scotland and the World. Under the heading Scotland to the World to Scotland, poets were invited to submit a poem, for display in the Museum and publication. Fifty-one poems from the over 260 received were selected by a panel of four: Dr Mario Relich of the Open University, Aonghas Macneacail, Gaelic poet, Catherine Lockerbie of *The Scotsman* and Jenni Calder of the NMS. The poems went on display to mark the first anniversary of the opening of the Museum of Scotland.

The poems here tell us about the experience of Scots who left Scotland. From governor general to GI bride, from missionary to man in the moon, this little volume covers many centuries and many miles in its exploration of exile. There are poems about arrivals as well as departures, about the rediscovery of Scotland after long absence, and about the threads that draw together different places, different peoples and different perceptions.

As with the first NMS poetry project, the posters were illustrated by students at Edinburgh Art College. We would like to thank them and Jonathan Gibbs of the Art College. We are also grateful to the members of the selection panel, to all the poets, to all those who made the display and the book possible, and to the Scottish Arts Council for their support of the project.

ORRA CLANS

Winds that blaw roun aa the warld
A rhymeless kip o raivelt threids
Richt orra kins an clans hae dirled –
Lord fairly! It sair duis wur heids!
Disna maitter gin we're Scot
Italian, Muslim, Roussian, Jew
Aa folks haes some bit anecdote
Shapes a tale o whaur we grew;
Past Scotland's trails, a fair lain spoor
O faimlies that hae link't the yirth;
Rede – as seid is strippt frae flooer –
Ae fuff! – the wind's o kittle worth.

Colin Donati Edinburgh

CRITH-THALMHAINN

Tha cian nan cian a-nis bho thàinig
gainneamh a Sahàra a Ghlaschu,
is tha creagan Leòdhais tòrr nas sine
na Tursachan Chalanais,
ach fhathast, chan eil sinn air ar glasadh
ri mòinteach is cladach,
no ann an taighean-prìosain
nam bailtean:
's tha crith-thalmhainn
gar sgapadh
gu rannan-ruadha an t-saoghail mhòir
's ar cainnt 's ar dualchas gar leantainn.

EARTHQUAKES

It was many ages ago
that the sand of the Sahara reached Glasgow,
and the Lewis rocks are much older
than the Callanish Giants,
but still we are not confined
to moor and seashore,
nor to the prisons
of the cities:
and an earthquake
scatters us
to the far edges of the great world,
with our language and our tradition going with us.

Ruaraidh MacThòmais (Derick Thomson) Glasgow

SAUMON RIN

Alevins kittled i the redd bi caller
water, leir the clarsach wimple o
chuckies i the rin, ken the tympanum
o dadded graivel, the arpeggio fuff
that skitters owre the lowp. Bonnilie they
jink, swippert, waukrife, gin, tyced bi the waff
o the muckle tide, they soum awa, smowts
wi a blinter o siller i thir een,
caad bi thir gangin-fins for faur-aff pairts.
They grow hale an fair, but aye thir hertsang
pous them back, the hertsang pous them back.

Muriel Ferrier Dundee

BORDERERS

Sometimes ancestors tread
south over Soutra Hill
follow Dere Street straight
through the old manse

drove their hopes and herds
hard through the season
crossing my Borders unseen
reddest dust on their feet

walking through stories
falling in with True Thomas
Tam Lin's Janet, passing
the unhired bondager

leaving no mention
of a pink moon's kiss –
oblivious to destination
kin of outgoer and incomer.

Alice Mitchell Oxton, Berwickshire

BLUT UND BODEN

The sword o Wallace licht i' his terrible hand,
Yeird barkit wi the bluid o's martyrdom:
Is thon yer wee bit hill and glen
Skail't ower five continents?
There is a tree in Fortingall that Pilate brocht,
Or sae they say.
Did he wander speirin aye 'and whit is truth?'
And ken it for a puir traiveller
Ower time and tide
'Or that we cry our historie wes scarce begun?
Puir Pilate mannie, historie has damn't ye
And yit I dout ye kent a thing or twa.

Gavin Sprott Edinburgh

KIRKMADRINE

Humpit stanes that mark a dawn,
beechen way tae a monk's-pate brae.
Dream o the barks that kirkmen sailed
oer rocky waves tae mak wet land
an fin a fowk bent on the deil.

Today we pray for sodgers far afiel.
At gloamin a shepherd's yew-carved
crook still questions a sombre lift.

John Hudson Kirkcudbright,
Dumfries and Galloway

SCHOTTEN

Chalmers, Cochranes, Cockburns, MacLeans, Weirs
left the rain at leith an aberbrothock
met weet snaw in the skagerrak's mooth
an flitted hoose an shore tae the baltic

in hansa's coorts, fairs an merkat touns
where the chapmen unrolled their packs like souls
the guid men o the guilds cauldly glowered,
drave oot the schotten mang the jews an poles

intil poland's hert an centuries' blood
tae kythe as surgeons, teachers, brewsters o beer
reckoners o five year plans – Czamer
Czochranek, Kabrun, Makalienski, Wajer

Matthew Fitt Coulter, Lanarkshire

INGAUNEES

This chaumert cairn kists bitties
O oor bricht an battert past –
A things that Scots hae keepit or drappit or lost
Or couldna tak wi them when they deed
Or went awa for guid.

Dootless there's ither grand ingaunees ootby
In Russia, India an sic fremmit fields
Whaur gangrel skelfs an shards o Scotland skinkle
Or gether stoor on shelves.
A feel fur thon wee Lewis keelies stuck in Lunnon
Goggle e'ed wi chowin the taps aff their shields,
Haimseek fur Norroway ower the faem.

Jim Alison Bridge of Weir, Renfrewshire

SETTLERS

Not so much Scotland small as the world –
at least wherever we connect with it.
For what's more forbidding than a blank page,
a passage dwindling to darkness? We move
from what we know through what we fear –
from byre, hearth, the rudiments of a home,
to a featureless plain, a forest's grim keep.

There, armed with names to tame the wilderness,
to mark it with whatever was taught
to us, we spin a future – in timber,
in stone. One, though not the only one:
for the records show we are twinned with ghosts.

Tom Pow Dumfries

WAVES OF EXILE

away ye go

        acroass thi wahtir

BIG FAT OCEANS

            make a   new life

      (write soon)

      make a new life (dont bother)

furget   n go   forward

        try harder

thi auld country

ay comin back

      a ghost in thi sea

      uvyir mind

            Jim Ferguson Glasgow

EMIGRANTS

(many years ago a relative of mine donated a rare African moth to
the Royal Museum, Edinburgh)

He saw a big moth land
and die on the clarted gable
of council flat. It was a graffiti rainbow
wider than a working man's hand.

Museum staff said it was rare:
African stowaway, blown airborne from
sweet-grass jungles. Yes, they
would be pleased to display it there.

Seeking work, emigrating, growing old,
he told me often of that moth,
which also crossed oceans,
to sleep in gardens strange and cold.

Tom Bryan Strathkanaird, Wester Ross

A SCOTS FAMILY, 1999

The young man, leaving by air:
a brisk wave at the turnstile,
a safe arrival on a sandy airstrip
where dawn and dusk are regular all year.

His sister, in London:
one among hordes of pretty post-graduates
picking fruit and books at Charing Cross,
not yet ready to return.

And now their parents:
suddenly not so young,
locking their car and walking down a pavement
very slowly to the polling station.

Sally Evans Edinburgh

THE EMIGRANT'S KIST

A set o' claes fur wearin',
a pair o' pots fur cuikin',
a muckle axe fur clearin',
a bag o' tools fur biggin',
   and the Wurd o' God
   fur baith dyin' and livin'.

Richard Love Edinburgh

A VERY BRIEF HISTORY OF THE DARIEN SCHEME

We turned up in the Tropics to chance our arm,
told the Indians we meant no harm,
and were very soon the best of pals
over bottles of whisky and hot mescal.
Then next we're on the forest floor,
trying to throttle conquistadors,
in plate armour to add insult,
but we thrashed them. What a result!
Then nobody turned up with fresh supplies,
so we died,
or spawned loads of freckled hottentots:
England at fault.

Hugh McMillan Dumfries

TWA TRIBES

Arapaho brave or Chief of Clan
Hunters on prairie or wind-lashed strath
Seekers of salmon, shooters of stag
Firewater blend: Scot, Native American.

Seanachie smoked peace with fierce Pawnee
With McGillivray of the Great Creek Nation
With 'White Bird' Ross of the Cherokee
Death chant: from Culloden to Wounded Knee.

Holy Ground from Glencoe to Idaho
from Argyll to bear and antelope.
White and Red brothers of Clearance and pain
MacDonalds gifted hope to Blackfoot and Crow.

Tom Bryan Strathkanaird, Wester Ross

HERE FOR THE COMPANY

This red dust would cling to exposed limbs.
Shrouded for doctoring in black suit,
hands and face are all the skin that shows.
Throat and sinuses coated with its acrid dryness,
mask the ward stink. Fourteen choleras today,
three jungle sores, the usual coughs and fevers;
much worse the ills of natives in the streets.
Some dried plants have arrived from the hills.
One I'm sure is new and Saleh, best of boys,
will paint it tomorrow. Now dined and brandied,
from verandah I look at Ganges, see the Tay.

Colin Will Mid Calder, West Lothian

HELLO CHIEF

John Ross, chosen leader o the United Cherokee Nation, born, Lookout
Mountain, Tennessee, 1790, deed, Washington, DC, 1866

History
Kent John Ross
Is politics an factions an spilt bluid
Ye wur chief o the United Cherokee Nation
A share thair cheekbanes, some bluid an mair.

Scart ayont the surface an see
Hoo aw the warld has taen Scots
Unner skin, in herts, in thocht an idea
Sae at hame this year celebrate
A muckle hamecumin:
The spirits fae aw pairts —
Mak fertile the hameland.

Andrew McNeil Dunfermline, Fife

The Governor General

Ali, bring me my churchwarden
and that fine brown bottle
which arrived this morning.

On the verandah
in this brief, loud dusk
I shall read Sir Walter.

May none of my satraps
rattle me with telegrams
as I journey north

with Edward Waverley
towards the harpings
of my own savage people.

Angus Calder Edinburgh

A SOLDIER OF THE BRITISH EMPIRE

The ocean is far behind, but yet he feels
the tug of its tide in this land locked place.
Night-time tears are just memories of salt
falling softly into the African lake.
They make no ripple but leave a bitter taste.

In the hot sun his arm swings a sword,
sweat dripping down onto a greedy ground.
He spits a storm of curses as he falls.
All around are other bodies;
lives seeping slowly into sand.
Blood turns into earth; stains the globe pink.

JE Natanson Kirriemuir, Angus

LIVINGSTONE AT VICTORIA FALLS

Though tumult here far exceeds
the Falls of Clyde,
because I know those
I can comprehend this.

Trees far outsoar our rowans
but principles of growth
leafing and fruiting
I understand from home.

A new tribe? Remembered friends
of childhood, echoes of Gaelic
convince me wholly
that I can talk to anyone.

Angus Calder Edinburgh

EXPLORATION OF THE INTERIOR, 1855

Dr Livingstone
in button mushroom topi,
scatters across Africa seeds
of civilisation and religion, claims
The Place of Thundering Waters
for his queen.
Victoria Falls? He smiles.
Ah no! Her crinoline balloons beneath
the flimsy parasol of Empire, then casts off
among the rising vapours to become a cloud.
But Mrs Livingstone,   perpetually pregnant,
declines to step forward for this experiment.

Jane Rawlinson Fetternear, Aberdeenshire

FINLAYSON IN TAMMERFORS

James Finlayson, Quaker, philanthropist,
engineer. In 1828 building a cotton mill
by Tammer Falls, creating wealth, creating

a working class. The Reds,
crushed in 1918. (Their last stand
was on Pispala Ridge, a mile from here.)

'Finland's Manchester' they say. But I think
of Scotland, a force frothing seawards, an angry
current of memory. Another red river.

Donald Adamson Tampere, Finland

THE COLOURIST

It wis the licht he desired:
The mellin pinks o the stane,
At Cassis, that myndit him o Mull;
But here wis flesh upon the bane,
And by unglowerin gods sae fired
That he lauched aff the hamewart pull.
A luve-bed in his studio
Celebrates auldest alliance:
A winnock apen to the sea
Lats in the Mediterranean dance
O air and virr and the echo
O aa that Scotland's yit to be.

Tom Hubbard Kirkcaldy, Fife

John Muir in Dunbar, 1893

'I am a Scotchman and at home again.'

Once, I mind it well, I climbed a Douglas fir
High in the Sierra, a storm was rising
And I squirrelled up that forest mainmast
So when it struck I'd feel what like it was
To be a storm-tossed tree. The wind blew
From the sea, a hundred and fifty miles away
But I swear I scented salt and I thought of here.
We are travellers together, trees and men;
They make their many journeys, and our own,
Away and back again, are only little more than
Tree-wavings. 'The evening brings aw hame',
It's said. I ken the truth of that. I feel it now.

James Robertson Kingskettle, Fife

RLS

The garden was unending to the child
but Mr Hyde was there, behind each tree.
A high bright sun smiled down; the breeze was mild;
the garden was unending. To the child
the trees were masts. He sailed across the wild
South Seas until he reached his final quay.
His Eden seemed unending; he was beguiled;
and Mr Hyde was there, behind each tree.

Jim C Wilson Gullane, East Lothian

MacIntyres at Gallipoli

1915: capture the Dardanelles;
secure sea route to Russia; remove Turkey
from the War; bridgehead Gallipoli.

Raised around Loch Long they travelled to the War
under distant colours. Scotty seconded
to the Aussies from Scottish Horse; Archie,
emigrant and farmer, with the Kiwis.
Each brother knowing nothing of the other.

Gallipoli, one hundred thousand dead,
chaos of blunders, misery – and chance.

Yet on one bloody beach the brothers meet
and our faded photo shows Scottish smiles.

Christopher Alderson Edinburgh

SOUTH GEORGIA, 2ND MARCH 1935

Gelatin trapped the silver
that ran through their fingers:
Calum, Angus, in seaboots,
flensing on
for as long as the print is fixed,
under the high salt hills
of Crytoiken
which might have been
West Loch Tarbert
in an industrialist's dream.

Ian Stephen Isle of Lewis

GI BRIDE

The images are salted in her head.
A cardboard suitcase. Passport. £10 note.
Two copies of her birth certificate.
Hand-sewn underwear in parachute silk.
A young girl jitterbugging up the gangplank
in Rita Hayworth curls and Persianelle coat.
The band playing *California Here I Come*
then *Auld Lang Syne*. Ship's siren. Gulls girning.
Her father's tears. She'd never seen him cry.
Her mother's sigh. *You've made your bed...*
Chums waving home-made flags; their voices fading.
The water widening between them.

Lydia Robb Dundee

HOME ICE

Deep into the foundation of a barn burnt down
he pitched slabs of slate from two gnarly fists
at a green knot of snakes I saw writhing there:
my grandfather, born in Dundee and orphaned
to a blasted frost-plain when diphtheria smashed
whatever his parents' dream had been. These
ramparts of a farm that took the boy in, French
family Celtic by design: what looked open was
a close-woven Möbius: he was a hired hand,
not a bairn, they'd loved only his rock-picker's
wrists with a stick on the pond. Hockey was what
warmed him, red and blue tartan of *les Canadiens*.

Mark Cochrane Vancouver, Canada

THE MAN IN THE MOON

He was only crescent-shaped sky-high folklore
when gene-juggling Armstrongs over-stepped a line
and cloned their sheep in Border raids,

then followed that with giant leaps overseas
to cultivate even greener pastures,
still indulging in their Scots traditions,

exaggerated, perhaps, when sending an offspring
up a ladder-rocket-capsule to first-foot the moon,
clutching a lump of its rock,

stepping across the pristine lunar threshold
and shaking dust off his boots –
moonstruck Neil metamorphosed into myth.

Marian Reid Alloway

Of doves and drums

Sam Campbell misses Jean a lot: a bomb
caught her as she shopped. He checks his farmhouse
locks before retiring with his bible.

He fears the city, loathes the towns: their drugs,
knee-cappings, ungodly shenanigans.
God, Crown and Ulster: binding Scottish roots
now lying raw, exposed; a bit like him.

His kitchen clock ticks beyond some deadline.
Craving past stabilities, he rages
in silence while the wings of fragile doves
beat louder than the loudest Lambeg drums.

Andrew McGeever

ORKNEY WRITES BACK

March 18th 1999

I spoke to Olive about thee Brigend butterflies
& it was Sandisons that owned them.
It was Lizzie's son Jim (ages with your father)
that took them home from China. Another Sandison
John by name sailed to South America
before the 1st War & died there with yellow fever
but Olive says it was Jim that took them home.
I mind a dog at the Brigend called Glen,
P&O Muir wad throw neeps & the dog fetched them.
His son Benjie went to New Zealand or Australia
I would need to find that out ...

J J Mary Hatakka Helsinki, Finland

Marzipan

Lübeck, winter '80 to '81;
students, we congregated at Tipasa,
named after Camus' absinthe-scented 'kingdom
of ruins', a quote from *Noces* concluding the menu

and there you were, who'd lived a few doors down
when we were kids, stranger than anything else
because you're not elsewhere, you're home. An attraction,
but really we never spoke the same language

and by the time I come to read those essays
it's all gone – you, those German idioms,
the very frontier – but not the marzipan
and not (according to various sources) Tipasa.

Ken Cockburn Edinburgh

PORT OF AUCKLAND

New Zealand Herald, 9.12.98: SHIPPING NEWS
From Sydney, 12.45pm: *Botany Bay*

Too far away, the ship swings in: my father's eyes
clock funnel, colours, movement, recognise *Bayline*
I listen to his pilot's voice quietly speak Scots:
I stood upon that bridge, along the London River
some other morning now too old to detail, but
close enough to know. The sun and stars and moon
make charts and keep us moving. On Orakei Jetty by
Bastion Rock, a spit reaching out from the near,
that seems as though it might go on forever into
blatant sky, we pause before we back along, and
watch her slowly clear. My young son takes my hand
suddenly scared, the wind he walks into will rise.

Alan Riach Hamilton, New Zealand

MO BHROGAN-DEIGHE

'S ann a dh' aona run
A bhios mi fagail mo bhrògan-deighe
Shios ann an shin ri taobh an dorais
A-staigh ann am baile mo dhaoine
Gus am faod mi èirigh is toirt às
A-mach à seo nuair a thig am fonn
Tarsainn air a' Chuan Siar, sìnte
Na *Raja batis* romham,
Cho leathann sin 's nach fhaic duine
Dà cheann an rud san aon àm,
Tarsainn air a' Chuan Siar
Air ais dhan a' Phòn Mhòr.

SKATES

I leave my skates down
Beside the door in my folks' place
Deliberately
So that I can get up and get the hell out of here
When the notion comes
Like a sound
Across the Atlantic, stretched out
Like a *Raja batis* before me,
So wide that you can't see
Its two extremities at once,
Across the Western Ocean
Back to Big Pond, Nova Scotia.

Rody Gorman Isle of Skye

Pilgrim Children

We were the children of emigrants
Brought to this un-home by our mother's journey;
We were only vaguely homesick
For her home, the focus of her heart.
Sometimes, like poorly printed images,
Parts of us were off-set, somehow
Our colours over-lapped our outlines.
And yet, inside, we were heroic,
With the quiet strengths
Of innocent, long-term prisoners,
And the inherited skills
That could make anywhere belong to us.

Katriina Hyslop Edinburgh

HERE AND THERE

Moray	Dallas	Texas
Ayrshire	Moscow	Russia
Old	Aberdeen	New Jersey
Fort	George	Washington
Livingstone	Blantyre	Malawi
Clan	MacKenzie	River
Gavin	Hamilton	Ontario
Bell's	Perth	Australia
Loch	Inver	Cargill
Scotland's	Dollar	Bill
Great	Glen	Miller
Scottish	Country	Music

Stuart B Campbell Portsoy

FROM SCOTLAND TO THE WORLD

this amber liquid, life's-blood
stirs the heart:

where freedom sings, duty-free
(duty-bound)

we bind

Scotland to the world
and back again

Anne Macleod Fortrose, Easter Ross

St Fillan's crook

A stranger to its native strath,
the tall foreigner, the coygerach,
was at the crowning of our kings,
raised the crest of all bright things.

Its keepers left for Eastern Canada
carrying the crook with them that far
to use its crystal as a cattle cure.
Where it dips, the water's pure.

From Canadian forests, settlers sent
the wanderer back into its element,
silver stripes crossing the Atlantic.
The brightness is inside the relic.

Valerie Gillies Edinburgh

LEGACY

Strange how a diminishing shoreline
Compels the level-headed
To weep for the intangible
And bask in forget-me-nots.

It is there in the music
In pibroch and old psalm tune –
Rage and passions seethe
For shipyard and empty glen.

As an exile I know
How to stand where I first stood.
The past nettles and keeps me
Half-submerged in the wreckage.

Maureen Macnaughtan Glenrothes, Fife

COMPLETIN DA CIRCLE

We nivver kent why you cam back fae Winnipeg
In sepia photos you lookit weel set up, ice skates
owre da airm, fur cep: a Shetland joiner wi a taste
fur stivvenin winters an skyscraper pay. Some said
you fell or lost a poase or hed ill luck in love
Somethin brook you, browt you silent hame. Some
plenishin man still be dere, sae gud your haands
Chance returned a grandson ta pick up da treed
an waeve hit in. His bairns ir true Canadians
Dey wear da kilt an proodly shaa wis foo ta dö
da sword dance, mak a saltire on da flör, step
neatly roond hits quarters ta complete da circle.

Christine De Luca Edinburgh

stivvenin – bitterly cold
poase – hoard
man – must

Pie owall Ho el

I stayed at the Pierowall Hotel on Westray
where a karaoke night was in progress,
islanders drinking themselves legless
and songward. Lauren and Sammo bought
two rounds and asked me out for coffee
next day. He tried guiding tourists but bills
went unpaid; either rigs or marine work
in Aberdeen. Lauren and six kids at home
with e-mail contact and maybe the hair-
dressing she'd trained for but never used.
I saw the wreck along the road before
I heard the news. One more change of career.

Gary Geddes British Columbia, Canada

THREADS

He severed his umbilical cord a second time, my great grand-
Father did, and sailed to America to be a painter of houses –
His life cut short by rheumatic fever; he had a son (who had a
Son, who had a son) who was I: a dot at the end of a line.

Today Scotland and America are connected by a long and
Winding cable that lies silent beneath the Atlantic waves –
I have followed this cable back, to stand dumbly with my
Hands in my pockets, listen for his frayed and shrinking voice.

I'd like to say I could plunge my hands in the ocean, uproot
The line, and with giant tugs, pull the lands together –
But we are connected by filaments more subtle than wires,
That summon us only with whispers, dissolve at our return.

Sean McGinty North Virginia, USA

ENTWINED

Guardians of India, idealists yet surgeons
or engineers, my ancestors to six generations
spent lives, sweat, tears, wives and children.
Home was a word in the heart, almost strange.

My medical grandpa: the only surviving child from ten.
My own three siblings died. How precious I was
to my parents! My mother's passion the birds and trees,
bright flowers that bloomed in the dust tra la.

India and Scotland are entwined like a Kashmir shawl
round my life. The knot cannot be unravelled but
can uncoil like a snake, start up like the brain-
fever-bird that disturbs any chance of rest.

Tessa Ransford Edinburgh

GENEALOGY

The stories great-grandfather told of our family
were only rumours of horse-thieves and an old man
with no birth-place. I may be decended from
an island man and woman fighting the elements
or the illegitimate children of kings. Until I
left the Midwest the tales were never questioned.
I settle into Glasgow's streets, create a language
of my own. I relearn the vowels of our surname
and find history in deaths and births. Patterns
emerge; son after son not speaking to father,
the long noses and silent women. I am the first
to return and I travel without map or compass.

Gerry Stewart Glasgow

TRACK

An old city poet speaks from the eye of a hurricane.
With only himself to thank for such a placeless space.

Back home in the west, merchant, priest, lawyer,
all had their place. Now people flee to their future

not seeing they cross track upon trek of ancestor
going where they have never gone before

through Himalayan chains, below Javanese volcano.
As this old bard harangues from his exiled space

his words vortex a poem. Gaelic, Scots, English,
pour from the weather eye of the hurricane.

At the same time where I am, the sun's rays
stroke my eyes at Ardnamurchan.

Neil mac Neil Sauchie, Clackmannanshire

Grampian Road

There was no gentling on those mountains,
no compromise to spawn a polite road
cut through layers of ancestral rock.
Browns and blacks dominated
confronted God. Now and then a white streak
gushed from hidden peaks to carve gullies,
split barren slopes. The shriek of white
repeated the intrusion of this road
told me I should not be there
had no rights on a private stage.
But now my stage is flat and the actors
speak a strange tongue-tied language.

Jennifer Footman Ontario, Canada

ANCESTRAL SLUMS

After checking out the home-place, doing
my graveyard rollcall of Pottingers,
Mowats and Houries, all paid-up members
of the exclusive underground club, I stopped
at the Brough of Gurness to put it all
in perspective. Between flagstone walls
a pale blue vinyl pup-tent had been pitched.
The camper, as blue with cold, was warming
hands over a propane stove he'd fired up
for tea. A Czech working at a health-care
facility in Inverness. Homesick, but
finding solidarity with the past.

Gary Geddes British Columbia, Canada

RETURN OF THE EMIGRANT ENGINEERS

Mechanisms? Oh aye, we were the boys for thaim.
Mechanise ye oot o sicht we cud, in thae days:
Railroad ye ower continents, steam ye tae Samoa,
Riverboat ye deep intae the bricht hert o Malawi.
Gie us a job - we'd feenish it; imagine a machine
Ye didna hae - we'd weld or rivet it fae whitiver
Wis tae haun. An nou ye want a kintra, *new*,
Earth-freenly, gleamin, iled wi non-sectarian ile,
Culturally multi-faceted but, whaur possible,
Recycled oot the auld material. That yer spec, eh?
Weill. Juist lea it wi us for a whilie wud ye?
There's naethin iver bate us yet.

James Robertson Kingskettle, Fife

Spar Cave, Isle of Skye

The pull beneath the water running over stone
revokes you, thresholds, links this living body
to inorganic pasts. 'The original unit survives
in the salt' breeze blowing now a world away,
within Spar Cave. I wish it could be clear, easily
as I lean down, push my hand down, through sheets
of running water, grip the quilted limestone, see
the water up to my wrist, a bangle of ice: solid,
petrified flesh, frozen desire, primal alteration
in the zones that lie inside us and the cave there
in the stone. So our love keeps, travels with us?
I'll carry it forever. I speak with your voice.

Alan Riach Hamilton, New Zealand

LERMONTOV'S YEARNING

From a translation by Victor Ramzes of a poem by Lermontov

Why can I not be those far geese from the Steppes
and range sky's freedom slowly westwards – west
to where tuim bields on mist-bound craigs in rain
haud banes o sodgers, my clan ancestors?
The wings would waft dust from a shield, brush
the clarsach till the strung calls rise to beat
in smoked roofbeams and I'd listen to them
die to the last echo. But my dreams are vain –
here by fate my birth was while my soul yearns
and a far sea heaves – I, last here of a line
of soldiers that must die in foreign snows –
why can I not be those far geese from the Steppe?

Colin Donati Edinburgh

Other titles available from NMS Publishing

Anthology series

Treasure Islands (Robert Louis Stevenson)	ed Jenni Calder
Scotland's Weather	ed Andrew Martin
Scottish Endings: Writings on Death	ed Andrew Martin
The Thistle at War	ed Helen McCorry

Scottish Life Archive series

To See Oursels	Dorothy I Kidd
Into the Foreground	Leah Leneman
Bairns	Iona McGregor

Scotland's Past in Action series

Getting Married in Scotland	Iona McGregor
Scottish Engineering: the machine makers	James L Wood
Scottish Bicycles and Tricycles	Alastair Dodd
Scotland's Inland Waterways	P J G Ransom
Farming	Gavin Sprott
Fishing and Whaling	Angus Martin
Spinning and Weaving	Enid Gauldie
Sporting Scotland	John Burnett
Making Cars	Alastair Dodds
Building Railways	James L Wood
Going to Church	Colin MacLean
Going to School	Donald Withrington
Leaving Scotland	Mona McLeod
Feeding Scotland	Catherine Brown
Going on Holiday	Eric Simpson
Scots in Sickness and Health	John Burnett
Going to Bed	Naomi Tarrant
Shipbuilding	James L Wood

Scottish Lives series (forthcoming)

Miss Cranston	Perilla Kinchin
Mungo Park	Mark Duffill
Elsie Inglis	Leah Leneman
Lochiel of the '45	John Gibson

General interest

Hieland Foodie	Clarissa Dickson Wright
Souvenirs	Godfrey Evans
Plastics: collecting and conserving	Anita Quye and Colin Williamson
Highland Gold and Silversmiths	G P Moss and A D Roe
Scottish Coins	Nick Holmes
Jewellery Moves: ornament for the 21st century	Amanda Game and Elizabeth Goring
The Scottish Home	ed Annette Carruthers
Tartan	Hugh Cheape
Precious Cargo: Scots and the China trade	Susan Leiper
The Scenery of Scotland	W J Baird
Collections in Context	Charles D Waterston

SPIRIT OF FLIGHT
compiled by Ian Gentle
1 901663 16 7, paperback, 64 pages, £5.99

Poems for all ages and every mood on the concept and experience of flight – from airshows and airports to skydivers and hot air balloons!

Celebrated aircraft and legendary events are also depicted in this compelling collection including the poignant *High Flight* by John Gillespie Magee, *Tangmere 1940* by Angus Duncain, to the mythological *Icarus* by Anne Macleod.

An airborne anthology to delight all fans of aviation, inspired by the historic collections at the Museum of Flight.

TRANSLATED KINGDOMS
compiled by Jenni Calder
1 901663 04 3, paperback, 80 pages, £5.99

Poignant poems reflecting more than a thousand years of Scotland and the sea.

The sea brought diverse peoples to Scotland's shores, and sent missionaries and emigrants to new worlds. Many have also depended on the sea for a living - mariners and merchants, fishermen and ferrymen, coastguards and lighthouse keepers.

Iain Crichton Smith, Norman MacCaig and Robert Louis Stevenson join many others in this moving testimony to the place of the sea in the Scottish imagination.

All titles available direct from NMS Publishing.
Please contact NMS Publishing Ltd, Royal Museum, Chambers Street, Edinburgh EH1 1JF.
tel: 0131 247 4026 fax: 0131 247 4012